99 Kids Jokes - Stampy Edition

JOHN JESTER

99 Hilarious jokes based on Stampy's favourite game.

What do Snow Golems wear on their head?
Why won't Endermen eat clowns?
Why don't Guardians eat penguins?

Find out the answers to these and many more hysterical jokes. You will never be able to play the game, without laughing out loud, ever again.

1. How do Creepers like their spawn eggs?

- Terri-fried!

2. What do you call Stampy's Pig that knows karate?

- A pork chop!

3. How many tickles does it take to make Squid laugh?

- Ten-tickles!

4. Why don't Spawn Eggs tell jokes?

- They'd crack each other up!

5. What do Snow Golems wear on their head?

- Ice caps!

6. If Stampy had 2 pet Wolves, he'd call them One and Two, coz if One died, he'd still have Two!

7. What do you call Stampy's Pig thief?

- Ham-burglar!

8. Did you hear about the Creeper's party?

- It was a blast!

9. What kind of music does a Sandstone Block like?

- Rock music!

10. What do you call Stampy's undercover Spider?

- A spy-der!

11. Why can't Stampy's Skeletons play church music?

- Because they have no organs!

12. Why won't Endermen eat clowns?

- They taste funny!

13. What do you get when you cross Stampy's cow with a trampoline?

- A milkshake!

14. What do you get from a Wither Skeleton?

- As far away as possible!

15. Why did half of Stampy's Chicken cross the road?

- To get to his other side!

16. Why was Stampy running around his bed?

- He wanted to catch up on his sleep!

17. What has four legs and goes "Oom, Oom"?

- Stampy's cow walking backwards!

18. What does an Ender Dragon become after it's one year old?

- Two years old!

19. Knock, knock.
- Who's there?
Stampy's cows say.
- Stampy's cows say who?
No silly, Stampy's cows say moo!

20. What 7 letters did Stampy say when he opened the chest and found it empty?

- O I C U R M T!

21. What kind of balls do Blazes play soccer with?

- Fireballs!

22. How do you spot a modern Cave Spider?

- He doesn't have a web, he has a website!

23. Which side of Stampy's chicken has more feathers?

- The outside!

24. What did Stampy's wolf say when he stepped on its foot?

- Aoooowwwwww!

25. What is Stampy's rabbit's favourite music?

- Hip hop!

26. What is a Zombie's least favourite room in Stampy's house?

- The living room!

27. What would you call Stampy's pet sheep if it had no legs?

- A cloud!

28. Why did Stampy's chicken cross the playground?

- To get to the other slide!

29. What do you get when you cross a mouse with Squid?

- An eektopus!

30. How does a Snow Golem travel to the portal?

- By icicle!

31. Stampy's pet wolf, Minton, ate all my shuttlecocks.

- Bad Minton!

32. What do you call Stampy's chicken in a shellsuit?

- An egg!

33. What do you get if you lay face down under Stampy's cow?

- A pat on the back!

34. What are the smallest rooms in Stampy's house?

- Mushrooms!

35. What makes Stampy's chickens laugh?

- A Comedi-hen!

36. Why don't Guardians eat penguins?

- They can't get the wrappers off!

37. Stampy put on a clean pair of socks every morning for a week.

- By Friday he could hardly put his shoes on!

38. What do Stampy's sheep do on sunny days?

- Have a baa - baa – cue!

39. What is a Zombie's favourite toy?

- A DEADY bear!

40. What has four legs and says OOM?

- Stampy's cow walking backwards!

41. Where do Stampy's sheep get their wool cut?

- At the BAAAbars!

42. What would happen if Pigmen could fly?

- The price of bacon would go up!

43. Why did Stampy's cow cross the road?

- To get to the udder side!

44. Where do you go to buy Zombies?

- The monSTORE!

45. What do Snow Golems like for dessert?

- I scream!

46. Why did the Creeper eat a Torch?

- He wanted a light lunch!

47. How many Pumpkin Seeds can you put in an empty chest?

- One! After that its not empty!

48. Where do Stampy's sheep go on holiday?

- The baaaahamas!

49. What did Stampy's pig say when he was sick?

- Call the ham-bulance!

50. What clothes does Stampy's house wear?

- Ad-dress!

51. Doctor, I feel like Stampy's pig.

How long have you felt like this?

About a weeeeeeek!

52. Who is a Snow Golem's favourite aunt?

- Aunt-artica

53. What time do Zombies wake up?

- At ATE o'clock!

54. What do you call an Iron Golem with no eyes?

- Ron Golem!

55. What day do Spawn Eggs hate most?

- Fry-day!

56. What's in the middle of an Ender Portal?

-The letter E!

57. What kind of make-up do Zombies wear?

- Mas-SCARE-a!

58. What newspaper does Stampy's cow read?

- The evening Moos!

59. What's brown, sounds like a bell, and comes out of a Stampy's cow backwards?

- Dung

60. Knock Knock
Who's there?
Coal Mine.
Coal Mine who?
Coal Mine number and find out!

61. What part of the minecart is the laziest?

- The wheels, because they are always tired!

62. What do you get when you cross a Zombie and Stampy's cat?

- A scaredy cat!

63. What did the Torch say to the other Torch?

- I'm going out tonight!

64. Why did Stampy's cookie go to the doctor?

- It was feeling crumby!

65. What do you call a Snow Golem in the desert?

- Lost!

66. Stampy is good friends with 25 letters of the alphabet.

- He doesn't know why!

67. There were two of Stampy's cows in a field. One said "moo", the other one said, "I was going to say that!"

68. What does Stampy's pig put on when it hurts itself?

- Oink-ment

69. What goes ha, ha, ha, clonk?

- An enderman laughing his head off!

70. What's a Ghast's favourite country?

- The Nether-Lands!

71. Where do Snow Golems keep their money?

- In snow banks!

72. How good is Stampy's favourite game?

- Top-Notch!

73. Why did Stampy call his Pig Ink?

- Because it kept running out of the pen!

74. Why did the Creeper cross the road?

- To get to the other Sssssssside!

75. What's the difference between Stampy and a book?

- You can shut a book up!

76. Where does Stampy take his Minecraft Pigs on Saturday afternoons?

- To the pig-nic!

77. A Skeleton walks into a bar and says, "Pint of cola and a mop!"

78. What happened when the Cave Spider got a new Minecart?

- It took it for a spin!

79. How does a Skeleton call his friends?

- On the tele-bone!

80. What should you do to a blue creeper?

- Cheer it up!

81. What's Stampy's pig's favourite game?

- Pig-pong

82. What do you call an Enderman with no arms or legs floating in a lake?

- Bob

83. Where does a Magma Cube sleep?

- Anywhere he wants to!

84. When do Zombies go to sleep?

- When they are dead tired!

85. Why did the Zombie visit Stampy in hospital?

- He wanted to learn some SICK jokes!

86. Why did Stampy get rid of his Chickens?

- Because they used fowl language!

87. What kind of fish did the Ghast catch?

- Spookled trout!

88. What do you get when you drop a Minecraft Pumpkin?

- Squash!

89. When is the only time a Zombie can make a Snow Golem?

- In the dead of Winter!

90. What do you call a Skeleton that won't do any housework at Stampy's house?

- Lazy-bones!

91. What game does Stampy's cow play at parties?

- Moo-sical chairs!

92. What did Stampy say to the Mushroom?

- You're a fun-guy!

93. What happened after the Creeper went to the French cheese factory?

- All that was left was de brie.

94. Teacher: "Stampy, what do Chickens give you?"
Stampy: "Eggs!"
Teacher: "Now what do Pigs give you?"
Stampy: "Porkchops!"
Teacher: "Great! And what does the Cow give you?"
Stampy: "Homework!"

95. Did you hear about the Villager with a broken left arm and broken left leg?

- Don't worry. He's all-RIGHT now!

96. How would Stampy's trees access the internet?

- They log-in!

97. What do Minecarts eat on their toast?

- Traffic jam!

98. What happens when you cross an Enderman with Stampy's cow?

- I don't know, but I wouldn't milk it!

99. What did the Villager say to the purple Creeper?

- Breathe stupid!